THE SECOND BOOK OF TENOR SOLOS

compiled by Joan Frey Boytim

G. SCHIRMER, Inc.

DISTRIBUTED BY

HAL•LEONARD®
CORPORATION
7777 W. BLUEMOUND RD. P.O. BOX 13819 MILWAUKEE, WI 53213

PREFACE

The eight volumes that comprise "The First Book of Solos" and "The First Book of Solos—Part II" were compiled to provide a great variety of song literature at the same basic level of difficulty for students at the beginning stages of voice study. The four volumes in "The Second Book of Solos" are designed to contribute to musical and vocal development at the next progressive level of study.

The majority of these songs require more vocal sophistication than those found in the earlier volumes. Singers using this set will be exposed to songs with wider ranges that require more vocal flexibility and vocal control, and that make greater use of the dramatic qualities of the voice. The student who can sing many of the songs in the "The First Book" and "The First Book—Part II" will be ready for the challenges found in "The Second Book of Solos."

The general format of songs remains the same as the previous collections, with a representative group of songs in English, Italian, German, and French from various periods of music history, as well as selected sacred solos. Added are several songs from Gilbert and Sullivan operettas and solos from the oratorio repertoire. Numerous pieces previously available only in single sheet form and many songs that for some time have been out of print are included.

I want to thank Richard Walters for encouraging the development of this practical song literature series. The twelve books, taken together, provide a comprehensive, inexpensive collection of 400 songs for the voice teacher and student.

Joan Frey Boytim

About the Compiler...

Since 1968, Joan Frey Boytim has owned and operated a full-time voice studio in Carlisle, Pennsylvania, where she has specialized in developing a serious and comprehensive curriculum and approach to teaching and coaching adolescent and community adult students. Her teaching experience has also included music and choral instruction at the junior high and senior high levels, and voice instruction at the college level. She is the author of the widely used bibliography, *Solo Vocal Repertoire for Young Singers* (a publication of NATS), and, as a nationally recognized expert on teaching beginning vocal study, is a frequent speaker and clinician on the topic.

CONTENTS

ALLELUIA!

Norah Phillips

17th Century

Piu tranquillo.

- ia!   O Lord, we pray that far and

wide._____   In ev-'ry heart love may a - bide. Al-le-

- lu - ia! Al-le-lu - ia! May strife and dis-cord ev - er cease,___

And grant to us Thy Bless-ed Peace, Al-le - lu - ia! Al-le-

all men joy and praise now bring, To

Christ our Ris - en Lord we sing, Al - le - lu - ia! Al - le -

- lu - ia! Al - le - lu - ia! Al - le - lu - ia! Al - le -

- lu - - - ia!

BE THOU FAITHFUL UNTO DEATH

from St. Paul

Felix Mendelssohn

AUTUMN EVENING

Arthur Maquarie

Roger Quilter

Where win - ter's winds will be un - known; So

poco rit.

deep thy rest,................. so deep thy rest...............

pp

Sleep on, my love, thy dreams are sweet,

poco cresc.

If thou hast dreams; the flow'rs I brought

I lay a - side for pass - ing feet, Thou need - est

nought,............... Thou need - est, need - - est

nought.............. The grapes are ga - ther'd from the

hills, The wood is piled, the song bird gone...............

The breath of ear-ly eve-ning chills:............... My

love, my love,.............. sleep on; My

love, my love, sleep on............

THE CALL

George Herbert

Ralph Vaughan Williams

Feast, as mends in length: Such a Strength, as makes _____ his

guest. _____ Come, my Joy, _____ my Love, my Heart: Such a

Joy, _____ as none _____ can move: Such a Love, as none _____ can

part: Such a Heart, as joys _____ in love.

CHRISTKIND
(The Christ Child)

Peter Cornelius
Edited, and text revised
by Henry Clough-Leighter

Peter Cornelius

or - gan, chant, and peal - ing bell.
Or - gel - klang und Glo - cken - schall

Christ - child
Christ-kind - lein

comes a - like _ to all, His arms _ en - fold both great _ and small. _
kommt zu Arm _ und Reich, die Gu - ten sind ihm al - le gleich. _

Then give Him
Dan - ket ihm

DEIN ANGESICHT

(Thy face so fair)

Heinrich Heine
Translated by Arthur Westbrook

Robert Schumann

lips a - lone are ro - sy - bright; Death soon will kiss them
nur die Lip - pen, die sind rot; bald a - ber küsst sie

cold and white,___ And quench the light of Par - a - dise, That
bleich der Tod.___ Er - lö - schen wird das Him - mels - licht, das

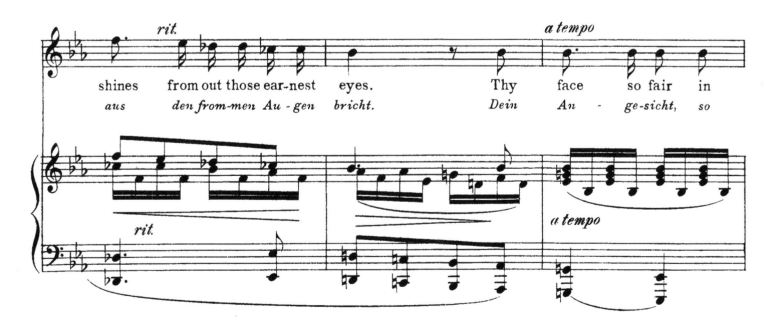

shines from out those ear - nest eyes. Thy face so fair in
aus den from - men Au - gen bricht. Dein An - ge - sicht, so

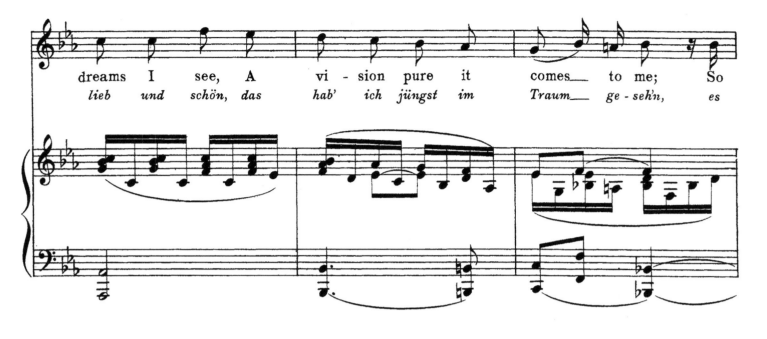

dreams I see, A vi - sion pure it comes___ to me; So
lieb und schön, das hab' ich jüngst im Traum___ ge - seh'n, es

gen - tle 'tis, so an - gel-fair, And yet so pale, so pale with
ist so mild und en - gel-gleich, und doch so bleich, so schmer - - zen -

care.
reich.

DER GANG ZUM LIEBCHEN

(The Watchful Lover)

Josef Wenzig
from a Bohemian folk song

Johannes Brahms

Es glänzt der Mond nie-der, ich soll-te doch wie-der zu
The moon is still show-ing, And I should be go-ing Once

mei- -nem Lieb-chen, wie mag es ihr geh'n?
more____ to see if my love will for - give;

Ach weh', sie ver- za-get und kla-get, und
But oh, she re- pels me, And chides me, and

kla - get, dass sie___ mich nim - mer im Le - ben wird seh'n!
tells me, She'll nev- -er see me as long as we live.

Tempo I

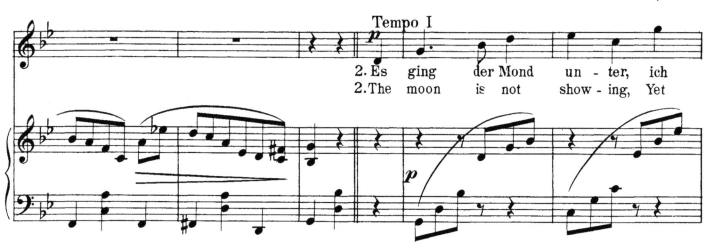

2. Es ging der Mond un - ter, ich
2. The moon is not show - ing, Yet

eil - te doch mun - ter, und eil - te, dass kei - ner mein Lieb - chen ent -
glad - ly I'm go - ing, I'm go - ing so no one may steal her a -

führt.
way;

animato

Ihr Täub - chen, o gir - ret, ihr Lüft - chen, o schwirret, dass
Ye doves, keep a - coo - ing, Ye breez - es, keep blow - ing, So

kei - ner mein Lieb - chen, mein Lieb - chen ent - führt!
no one may steal her, may steal her a - way!

DIE FORELLE

(The Trout)

Franz von Schober
Translation by Theodore Baker

Franz Schubert

tin - ues round a - bout,   The wretch will nev - er cap - ture My
dacht' ich, nicht ge - bricht,   so fängt er die Fo - rel - - le mit

bon - ny lit - tle trout,   Thou'lt nev - er catch thou var - let, My
sei - - ner An - gel nicht,   so fängt er die Fo - rel - - le mit

bon - ny lit - tle trout.
sei - - ner An-gel nicht.

What did the bus - y bod - y   A
Doch end - lich ward dem Die - - be

fraid to lose his prey,   He made the wa - ter
die Zeit zu lang,   Er macht das Bäch - lein tü - ckisch

DREAM-LAND

Christina Rossetti

Ralph Vaughan Williams

Where sun - less riv - ers weep___

___ Their waves in - to the deep,___ She sleeps a charm - èd sleep: A -

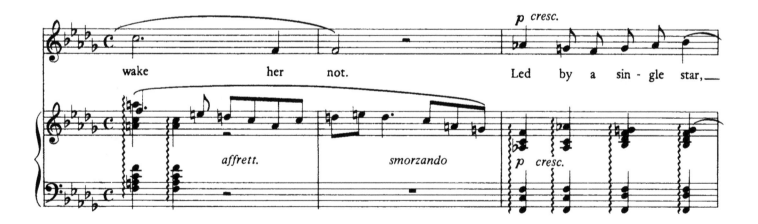

wake her not. Led by a sin - gle star,___

affrett. *smorzando*

She came from ver - y far ___ To seek, where shad - ows are, Her ___

pleas - ant lot.

affrett.

Poco animando

She left the ros - y morn, She left the fields of corn, For twi - light cold and

lorn And wa - ter - springs.

Through sleep, as through a veil, ___

poco riten.

She sees the sky look pale, ____ And hears the night - in - gale That sad - ly

colla voce

Tempo I

sings.

Molto tranquillo

Rest, rest, a per - fect rest Shed o - ver brow and breast;

p ma pesante

poco mf

Her face is toward the west, The pur - ple land. She

mf poco

can - not see the grain Rip - 'ning on hill and plain, She can - not

feel _____ the rain Up - on her hand.

Rest, rest, for ev - er - more Up - on a mos - sy shore;

Rest, rest at the heart's core Till time shall

cease: Sleep that no pain shall wake; Night that no

morn shall break Till joy shall o - ver -

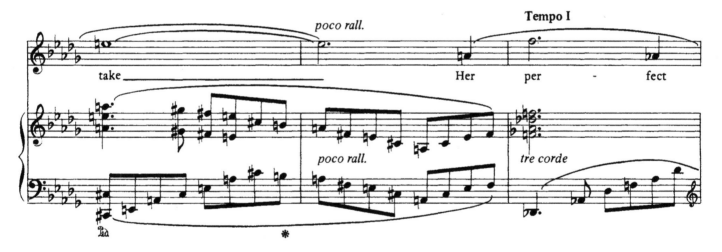

take _____ Her per - fect

peace. _____

THE GREEN HILLS O' SOMERSET

Fred E. Weatherly

Eric Coates

there   we kissed and   said good-bye   Be - side the kirk - yard

wall,   And the   song the black - bird   sang to us   Was—

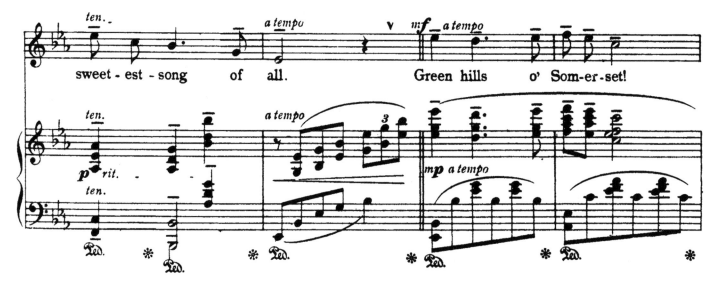

sweet - est - song   of   all.   Green hills   o' Som - er - set!

Green   hills   o'   Som - er - set!   When   shall   we

sha - - dows kiss the wav - ing grass, Be -

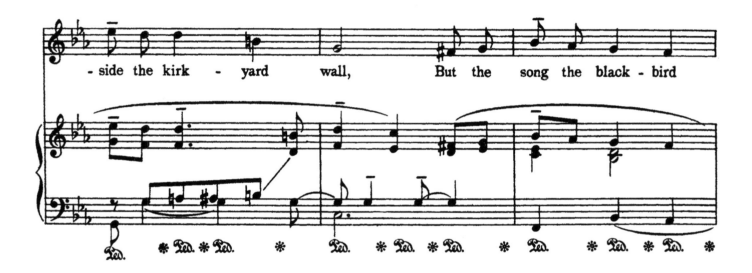

- side the kirk - yard wall, But the song the black - bird

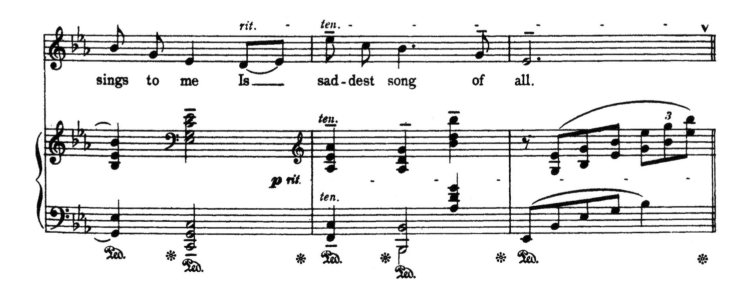

sings to me Is___ sad - dest song of all.

Green hills o' Som-er-set! Green hills o' Som-er-set!

No more we walk by you— Green hills, no more!

FAIR HOUSE OF JOY

Words Anonymous

Music by
Roger Quilter
Op. 12, No. 7

Fain would I change that note To which fond Love hath charm'd me Long, long to sing by

rote, Fan-cy-ing that that harm'd me: Yet when this thought doth

come 'Love,_____ Love is the per-fect sum Of all de-

-light!' I have no o-ther choice Ei-ther for pen or

voice To sing or write.

dolce amoroso.

O Love! they wrong thee much That say thy

a tempo.
P *dolce amoroso.*

sweet is bit _ ter, When thy rich fruit is

such As no _ thing can be sweet _ er.

cresc.

Fair house of joy and bliss, Where tru _ est, where tru _ est plea _ sure

cresc.

Ped.   *

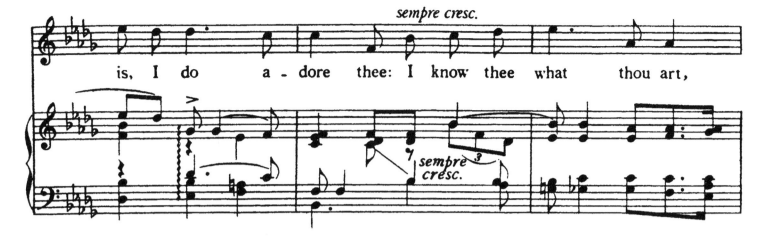

is, I do a - dore thee: I know thee what thou art,

I serve thee with my heart, And fall be - fore thee,

And fall be - fore _____ thee.

FREE FROM HIS FETTERS

from The Yeoman of the Guard

W.S. Gilbert

Arthur Sullivan

heart! Bound to an un-known bride

For good and ill; Ah, is not one so

tied_____ A pris - - 'ner_ still, A pris - 'ner_

still? Ah, is not one so tied_____ A

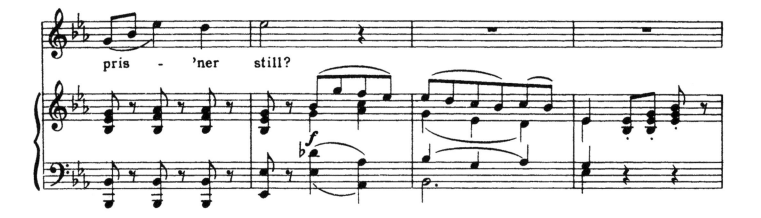

pris - 'ner still?

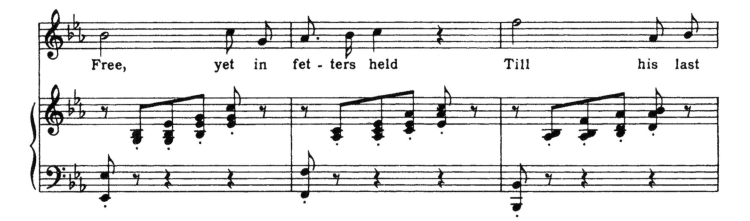

Free, yet in fet - ters held Till his last

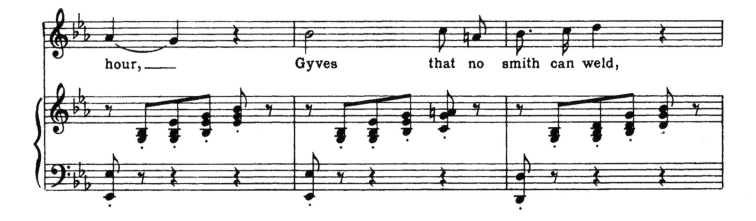

hour, ___ Gyves that no smith can weld,

No rust ___ de - vour! Al - though a mon-arch's hand

Had set him free, Of all the cap-tive band ___ The

sad - - dest he, The sad - - dest he!

dim.

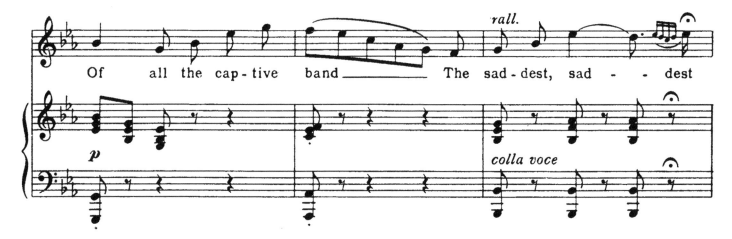

Of all the cap-tive band ___ The sad - dest, sad - - dest

rall.

p

colla voce

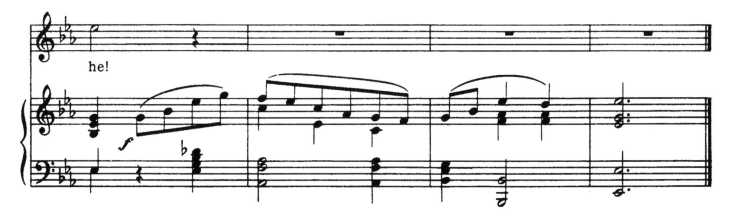

he!

f

FRÜHLINGSTRÄUM

(Spring Dreams)

Wilhelm Müller

Franz Schubert

Printed in the U.S.A. by G. Schirmer, Inc.

ra-vens were croaking o'er-head; And all was cold and dis-mal, The
schreien die Ra-ben vom Dach; da war es kalt und fin-ster, es

ra-vens were croaking o'er - head. But on the window-
schreien die Ra - ben vom Dach. Doch an den Fenster-

Lento.

pane there Who drew all those leaf-y plumes? But on the win-dow pane there Who
schei - ben, wer mal-te die Blät-ter da? doch an den Fen-ster-schei - ben, wer

drew all those leaf - y plumes? Why need ye laugh at the dream-er, Whose
mal-te die Blät-ter da? Ihr lacht wohl ü - ber den Träu-mer, der

gar-den in win-ter blooms, Whose gar-den in win-ter blooms?
Blu-men im Win-ter sah, der Blu-men im Win-ter sah.

lone - ly here I'm sit - ting, Re - call - ing my dream a - gain.
sitz' ich hier al - lei - ne und den - ke dem Trau - me nach.

A - gain mine eyes are clos - ing, Yet throbs my heart a -
Die Au - gen schliess' ich wie - der, noch schlägt das Herz so

main; A - gain mine eyes are clos - ing, Yet throbs my heart a -
warm; die Au - gen schliess' ich wie - der, noch schlägt das Herz so

main: Will ev - er ye leaves turn_ green then? Shall I e'er my sweet - heart em -
warm. Wann grünt ihr Blät - ter am Fen - ster, wann halt' ich mein Lieb - chen im

brace? Shall I e'er my sweet - heart em - brace?
Arm? wann halt' ich mein Lieb - chen im Arm?

Lento.

I'LL SAIL UPON THE DOG STAR

(A Fool's Preferment)

Henry Purcell

stars pluck from their orbs, too, the stars pluck from their orbs, too, And crowd them in my bud-get!

And whe-ther I'm a ___ roar -

- ing boy, a roar -

- ing boy, Let all, _____ let_ all the_ na - tions judge it.

THE LORD IS MY SHEPHERD

Samuel Liddle

LONG AGO

Edward MacDowell

MIT EINEM GEMALTEN BAND

(With a Painted Ribbon)

Ludwig van Beethoven

NATURE BEYOND ART

Thomas Arne

Still to be neat,

Still to be drest,___ As you were go - ing to___ a

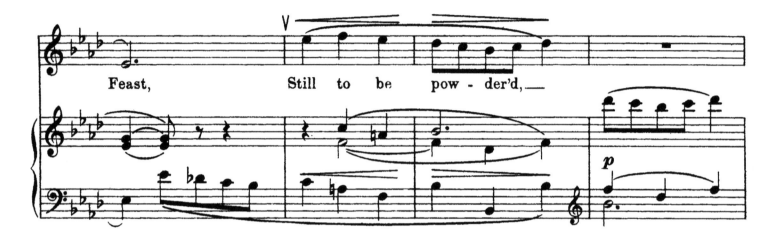

Feast, Still to be pow - der'd,___

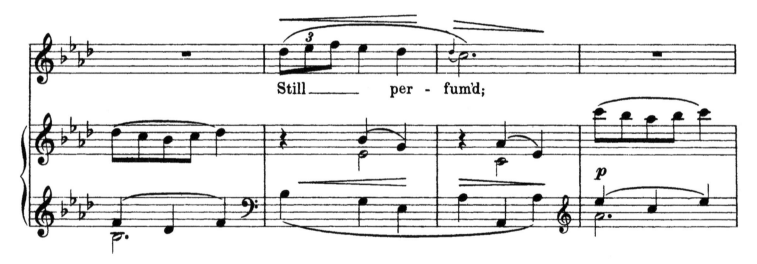

Still___ per - fum'd;

Ah, La - dy, 'tis___ to be___ pre - sumed, Tho'

arts hid cau - ses, are___ not - known by

Nat - ure, All is not your___ own by

Nat - ure, All is not___ your own.___

Give me a look, Give me a face___ That makes sim -

pli - ci - ty___ a grace; Robes love-ly flow - ing,

hair___ as free;

Such sweet ne - glect more takes with

me, Than all the glar - ing modes___ of

Art, That strike my eyes but not ___ my

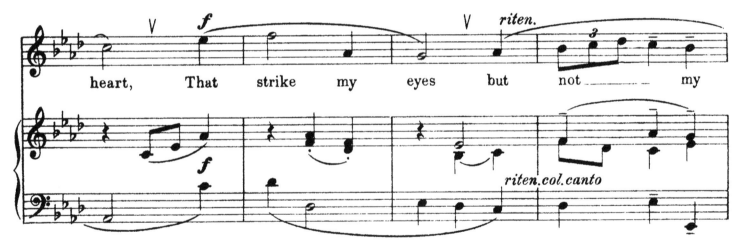

heart, That strike my eyes but not ___ my

heart.

MY LIFE'S DELIGHT

Thomas Champion

Roger Quilter

loves no de - lay; thy sight

poco cresc.

— The more en - joyed, the more di - vine. O come,

— O come, and take from me The pain of being de - priv'd of

poco rall.

poco rall.

thee.

poco rit.

mf a tempo.

Thou all sweet - ness dost en - close,

Like a lit - tle world of bliss: Beau - ty, beau - -

- - ty guards thy looks: the rose___

___ In them pure and e - ter - nal is. Come

then, come then! O come, and make thy

flight As swift, as swift to me

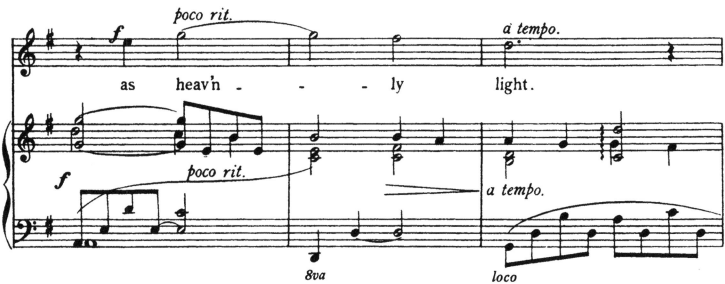

as heav'n - - ly light.

O THOU BILLOWY HARVEST-FIELD!

A. Tolstoi
English version by
Henry G. Chapman

Sergei Rachmaninoff, Op. 4, No. 5
(1893)

O thou bil - low - y har - vest - field of _____ grain! _____

were ye scat - tered, __ O my __ dreams! __

Yet wher - e'er _____ one a -

mong _____ you has __ fall'n to earth,

There have sprang from the soil weeds of mis - er - y, There has flour - ished the

bit - ter - est heart's dis - tress! Ah!

Con Moto

Ah!

THE PLAGUE OF LOVE

William Whitehead

Thomas Arne

can't tell how The pleas-ing plague stole on me! And

yet,— I swear,— I can't tell how— The pleas-ing— plague stole

on me.—

Her voice, her smile might give— th'a-larm, 'Tis

both per - haps has won me, 'Tis both per - haps has

won me, And yet, I swear, I can't tell how The

pleas - ing plague stole on me; And yet, I swear, I

can't tell how The pleas - ing - plague stole on me.

ORPHEUS WITH HIS LUTE

from Henry VIII
by William Shakespeare

Ralph Vaughan Williams

Printed in the U.S.A. by G. Schirmer, Inc.

mu_sic plants and flow'rs ev _ er sprung as sun and

showers .... there had made a last _ ing spring.

Ev _ ry _ thing that heard him play, ev_en the bil _ lows

of the sea, hung their heads, and then lay by. In sweet

mu _ sic is such art, Kill _ _ ing care and

grief............. of heart, fall.....................................a _ sleep, or

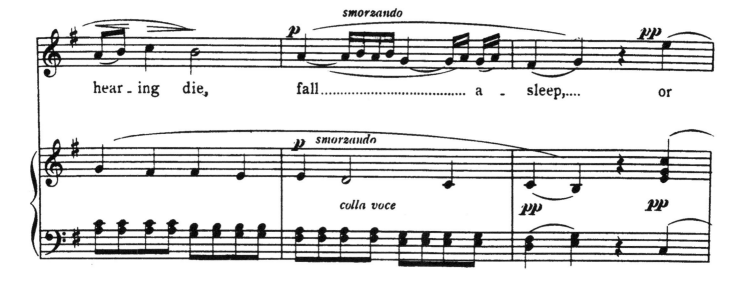

hear_ing die, fall................................. a _ sleep,.... or

hear - - - - - ing die.

OUVRE TES YEUX BLEUS

(Open Thy Blue Eyes)

Paul Robiquet
English version by Willis Wager

Jules Massenet

mour.   L'au-ro - re.é-pa-nou-it la ro - se:
love.   The dawn   un-folds the bud-ding ros - es;

Viens a - vec moi   Cueil-lir   la mar-gue-ri-te é -
O   come   with me   To cull   the dai-sies it dis-

clo -   se.   Ré - veil - le - toi!
clos -   es.   I   call   to thee!

Ré - veil - le - toi!
I   call   to thee!

Ou- vre tes yeux bleus, ma mi- gnon - - - ne; Voi - ci le
O- pen thy blue eyes to the dawn - - - ing, Now high a-

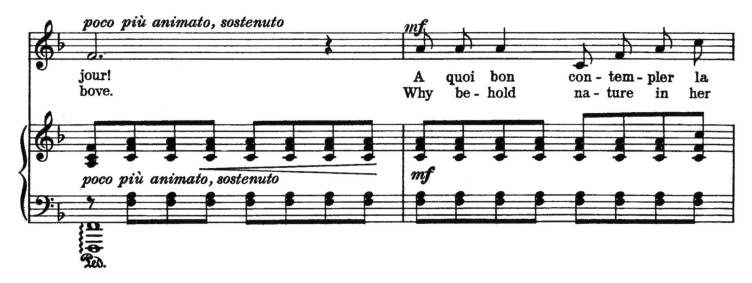

jour! A quoi bon con - tem - pler la
bove. Why be - hold na - ture in her

ter - re Et sa beau - té? L'a-
splen - dor With rap - tured gaze When

mour est un plus doux mys - tè - - re Qu'un jour d'é-
love's a mys - t'ry far more ten - - der Than sum - mer

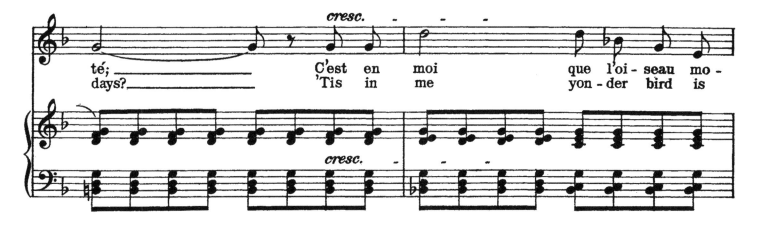

té;_____ C'est en moi que l'oi-seau mo-
days?_____ 'Tis in me yon-der bird is

du - - - le Un chant vain - queur,_____
call - - - ing With all its art,_____

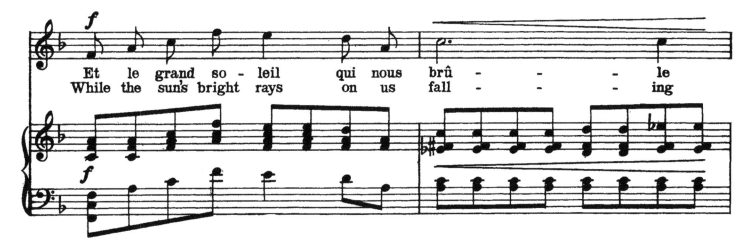

Et le grand so - leil qui nous brû - - - le
While the sun's bright rays on us fall - - - ing

Est dans mon cœur!_____
Fill all my heart!_____

POLLY WILLIS

Thomas Arne

At - tend,__ ye nymphs and tune__ -ful swains, Who in per - sua - -sive lul - ling strains Of

Chlo - e sing, or Phyllis, or Phyllis; Of Chlo - e sing, or

Phyllis; Tho' rude my voice and mean my verse, Up-

raid me not, while I _____ rehearse The charms of Pol - ly

Wil - lis, Pol - ly Wil - lis, The charms of Pol - ly Wil - lis.

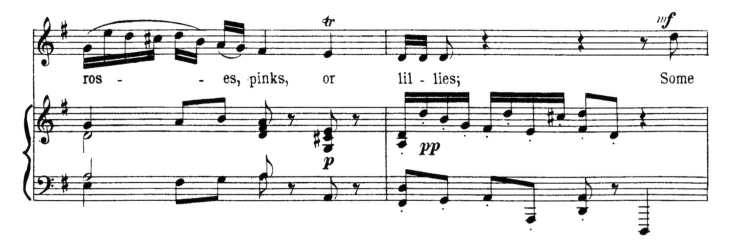

common beau - ties they may hit, But sure_ no sim - i -

le _ e'er can fit The charms of Pol - ly Wil - lis, Pol - ly Wil - lis, The

charms _ of Pol - - ly _ Wil - lis.

She's

not _____ as Ve - nus on _____ the flood, _____ Nor

as she once on I - da_ stood, Nor

mor - - - -tal Am - a - ryl - lis, Am-a-ryl - lis, Nor

mor - - - - -tal_ Am - a - ryl - lis. Frame

all that's beau - teous, gay, and fair, With

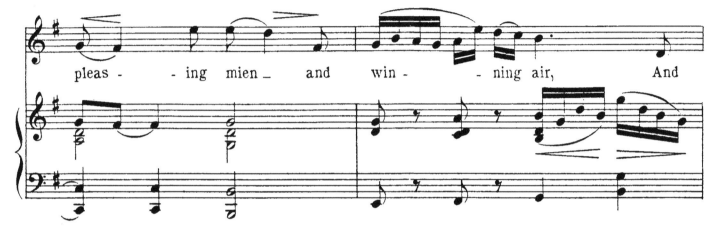

pleas - - ing mien _ and win - - ning air, And

that _____ is Pol - ly Wil - lis, Pol - ly Wil - lis, And

that _____ is_ Pol - ly _ Wil - lis.

ROSE CHÉRIE, AIMABLE FLEUR

(Rose Sweet and Cherished)

English version by Joan Boytim

André-Ernest-Modeste Grétry

See_ how_ it _ blos-soms, this_ ten-der_ flow-er! Ah,
Qu'elle est fleu - ri - e! · Qu'elle est fleu - ri - e! Voy-

flow'r di - vine,— Be Al - - - ways mine!
ez ma soeur,— ma chè - - re soeur!

Dear Rose so cher - ished,— Dear Rose so cher - ished,—
Ro - se ché - ri - e,— Ro - se ché - ri - e,—

Come _ to my heart._ Dear Rose so _
Viens _ sur mon coeur! _ Ro - se ché -

cher-ished, _____ Come __ and __ gent - ly__
ri - e, _____ Viens __ du __ moins __ mou -

die on_ my_ heart. _ Dear Rose so cher-ished, _____
rir sur_mon_ coeur! Ro - se ché - ri - e, _____

Come_ and_ gent - ly __ die on __ my __ heart, gent - ly __
Viens_ du moins_ mou - rir sur___ mon __ coeur! Viens mou -

die on __ my __ heart!
rir sur__ mon_ coeur!

TURN THEE TO ME

Antonín Dvořák

great are the sor-rows of my heart; bring me out of my dis-

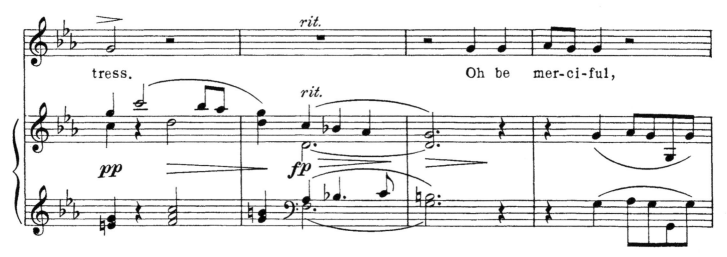

tress, bring me out of my dis-

tress. Oh be mer-ci-ful,

look on my sor - row, see mine af-flic-tion and for - give me all my

wick - ed -ness. Oh, keep my soul in safe - ty and de-
liv - er me. Let me nev - er be con - found - ed
for my hope is in Thee,
for my hope is in Thee, __ in Thee.

LE SOIR
(Evening)

Michael Carré
Translated by Isabella G. Parker

Ambroise Thomas

wait - - ing that heav - en The fresh dew may bring._____
tend_____ la ro - sé - e Qui tom - be des cieux._____

Cool - er winds are_____
La cha - leur_ s'a -

blow - ing, Blest_____ re - lief be-stow - ing. The birds sweet-er
pai - se, On_____ res-pire à l'ai - se, L'oi-seau chan-te

sing, The birds_____ sweet-er sing._____
mieux, L'oi - seau_____ chan-te mieux._____

dim.

pp

Shad - ows, deep de - scend - - ing, From the trees are
Le feuil - la - ge som - - bre Cou - - vre de son

bend - ing___ Where fond lov - ers meet.
om - bre___ Les a - mants heu - reux

While the star-beams ten - - der
Et plus d'une é - toi - - le,

pp

SPIRATE PUR, SPIRATE

Stephano Donaudy

Spirate pur, spirate
attorno a lo mio bene

Blow then, blow
about to my beloved·

Printed in the U.S.A. by G. Schirmer, Inc.

lo ___ mio be - ne, ___ au - ret - te, e v'ac - cer -

ta - te ___ s'el - la nel cor mi tie - ne, ___

p leggero

___ s'el - la nel cor mi tie - ne ___ Spi -

pp

aurette, e v'accertate   *breezes, find out*
s'ella nel cor mi tiene   *if she holds me in her heart*

Spirate, aurette!

Blow, breezes!

Se nel suo cor mi tiene,
v'accertate aure beate,
aure lievi e beate!

If she holds me in her heart,
find out, blessed breezes
breezes light and blessed!

-ra - te pur, spi - ra - te _____ at - tor - no a lo ___ mio

p a tempo   *p*   *leggero*

be - ne, _____ au - ret - te, e v'ac - cer - ta - te _____

p leggero

s'el - la nel cor mi tie - ne, _____ s'el - la nel cor mi

tie - ne   Spi - ra - - - te,

pp

pp

Spirate pur, spirate   *Blow then, blow*
attorno a lo mio bene   *about to my beloved*
aurette, e v'accertate   *breezes, find out*
s'ella nel cor mi tiene   *if she holds me in her heart*

spi - - ra - te, spi - ra - te pur, spi - ra - -

- te, au - ret - - te!

Spirate pur, aurette!　　　*Blow then, breezes!*

TOTAL ECLIPSE

George Frideric Handel

VAGHISSIMA SEMBIANZA

(O, Likeness, Dim and Faded)

Stephano Donaudy

Vaghissima sembianza d'antica donna amata

O charming image of an ancient woman

Printed in the U.S.A. by G. Schirmer, Inc.

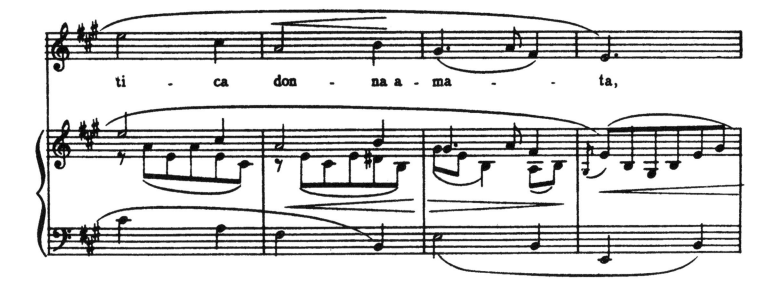

ti - ca don - na a - ma - - ta,

chi, dun - que, v'ha ri - trat - - ta

con tan - ta si - mi - glian - - za ch'io

chi, dunque, v'ha ritrata con tanta simiglianza
ch'io guardo

who, then, has been painted with so much similitude
that I loook

e parlo, e credo
d'avervi a me davanti
come ai bei di d'amor?

and speak and believe
to have you before me
as in the beautiful days of love?

ca - ra ri - mem - bran - za che in cor mi

s'è de - sta - ta si ar - den - te v'ha già

fat - ta ri - na - scer la spe -

La cara rimembranza
che in cor mi s'è destata
si ardente v'ha già fatta
rinascer la speranza,

The dear memory
that in my heart is awakened
so ardent here has now made
my hope to be reborn.

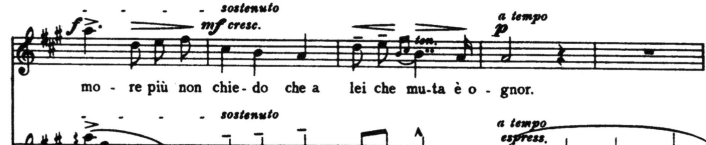

che un bacio, un voto, un grido d'amore
più non chiedo che a lei che muta é ognor.

*so that a kiss, a pledge, a cry of love
I ask not more but of her whose silence is forever.*

WHEN FIRST MY OLD

from Trial by Jury

WHEN FIRST MY OLD

from Trial by Jury

W. S. Gilbert

Arthur Sullivan

Printed in the U.S.A. by G. Schirmer, Inc.

used ___ to mope, ___ and sigh, ___ and pant, Just like a love - sick
last, ___ one morn - ing, I ___ be-came An - oth - er's ___ love - sick

boy.
boy.

2. But

WHITHER MUST I WANDER?

Robert Louis Stevenson

Ralph Vaughan Williams

rain and my roof is in the dust. Lov'd of_wise men was the shade of my roof-tree, The true word of wel-come was spo-ken in the door: Dear days of old_with the fa-ces in the fire - light; Kind folks of old, you_come a-gain no more.

Home was home then, my dear, full of kind-ly fa - ces, Home was home then, my dear,_

hap-py for the child.   Fire   and the win-dows bright glit-tered on the moor -

- land;   Song, tune-ful song, built   a pa-lace in   the wild.

Now   when day dawns on the brow of the moor-land,   Lone stands the house and the

chim-ney-stone is cold. Lone let it stand now the friends are all de-part -

- ed, The kind hearts, the true hearts, that loved the place of old.

Spring shall come, come a-gain, call-ing up the moor-fowl, Spring shall bring the sun and rain,

bring the bees and flow - ers; Red shall the hea-ther bloom o-ver hill and val -

-ley,   Soft   flow the stream through the e-ven flow-ing hours.

Fair the day_ shine as it   shone on my child - hood; Fair shine the day   on the

house with o - pen door.   Birds come and cry there and twit-ter in the chim -

-ney,   But I   go for e - ver and come a-gain no more.